The Picker's Secret Money Making Guide

To Thrifting, Flea Markets, and Collectables

By L.T. Bronson

Copyright © 2024 by L.T. Bronson

All rights reserved.

The Picker's Secret Money Making Guide

L.T. Bronson

No part of this book may be reproduced or used in any manner without written permission of the copyright owner except for the use of quotations in a book review.

This publication is designed to provide accurate and authoritative information in regard to the subject matter covered. The advice and strategies contained herein may not be suitable for your situation. You should consult with a professional when appropriate. Neither the publisher nor the author shall be liable for any loss of profit or any other commercial damages, including but not limited to special, incidental, consequential, personal, or other damages.

Book Cover by L.T.Bronson

Illustrations L.T. Bronson

First eBook edition 2024

Contents

Introduction: You Too Can Be A Profitable Picker...Or Great Collector!

Chapter 1: Where To Find The Gold

Chapter 2: The Items That Sell

Chapter 3: Strategies For Selling

Chapter 4: Setting Up And Buying At The Flea Market

Chapter 5: Buyer (And Picker) Beware

Chapter 6: What It Takes To Survive

Epilogue: The Treasure Hunt Continues

Introduction: You too can be a profitable picker...or a great collector!

This book is written in a way that allows you to jump right in and start making money. Whether you are looking to buy and sell on eBay or the flea market, or you just want to have the edge on the competition as a buyer or collector, this book is for you—this book cuts right to the chase. You have probably seen shows like *American Pickers, Storage Wars, Chip and Joanna Gaines' Magnolia, Flip or Flop*, and countless others, but they just scratch the surface. They show up at the scene ready to magically buy, but how did they make the connections? I wrote this book as if we were sitting down together in a consultation, and I am passing on everything I know about the *picker biz*.

At times, I'll be brutally honest about what you can expect, and this will prepare you, and keep you from getting scammed, rammed, and shammed. I will not only give you the tricks of the trade, but I will also give you solid examples and strategies of ways to make money. No matter whether your thing is vintage clothing, toys, glassware, antiques, electronics, coins or literally anything else on the world market today, the principles and secrets in this book can be applied across the board.

I have decided that the time has come to put everything I know about "making it" in this biz down own paper. Some people will definitely be angry at me for giving away the money-making secrets, but hey, who cares, I believe even if some people read this book and learn the tricks of the trade, they still may not take the leap and start making money or catching good deals from it.

We have all heard the stories of Davey Crocket or other pioneers surviving off the land and making their place in the world off of trapping, self-sufficiency, and good ole American spirit. One of the things that draws so many people to the flea market picker way of life, is the possibility of being their own boss, and not having to answer to anyone else. Anyone who's ever spent time in a cubicle, warehouse, or fast-food job, knows all too well that no matter how hard we work, we can never seem to have the life that the owner has—we are basically just pawns in their game, making them wealthy, while we just punch a clock. Unless you were born into wealth, there are only several (legal) ways to rise above in this world; Go to school, learn a trade, or start a business. None of these are guaranteed by the way, in this day in age, and I only mention that because, even with a decent salary, so many people are turning to a "side hustle" to make ends meet. And that's what this book is about, it can either be a "side deal" or it can be a way of life that brings you to a new level, the choice is yours. You may just use this info to get ahead of the other buyers out there for your own collecting purposes, and that's ok too. It all comes down to a few things in my opinion: How much you want something, how you apply the techniques in this book, what you want to achieve, and yes, I do believe it can be fate and destiny as well.

The truth is, you can make a living off this way of life—it doesn't take a certain type of person, anyone can do it. You can start small and work your way up depending on your available cash that you have to invest; or if you have a lot of money up front, as with all things, you can make bigger purchases that bring about larger paybacks and profit margins (we'll talk more about that later).

I have been involved in the antique, flea market, thrift store, collectible market for over 30 years. As a little boy, my grandfather abandoned his family and left my grandmother to fend for herself...and her 7 children. A few of her friends started by selling items, and baking goods that they took to a local flea market, this turned into a way for them to provide for their families, and they then branched out into buying antiques, and opening their own store, which allowed them to feed their kids, and pay their rent. I learned many tricks of the trade from these women, and by the time I was a teenager, me and my friends were camping out in our cars in the flea market parking lot at 3am, catching some sleep on a Friday night, and waking up at sunrise to set up our tables full of junk. Many decades later, many of these same friends now own multiple toy/collectible stores, and one even became an auctioneer, and runs his own auction house.

Some people get involved with collectables just for fun—to be social and sell/trade a few things, and others make it their way of life. When I was 7 years old, I was walking down the street with a soda and candy bar in my hands from the local corner store. It was a summer morning, and I could feel the warm sun on my face— it also happened to be garbage day. As I walked down the street like I had a thousand other times, I noticed out of the corner of my eye, an old tin Marx Fort Apache Playset sitting right on top of the black garbage bags to my left. If you've never seen one before, the old Marx playsets were about the size of a suitcase, and they opened up to hold all the small plastic figures and accessories inside. I started to feel my heart race, and I scanned around me to see if anyone was in their front yards—nope, the coast was clear. Up until that moment, I had never seen anything worth grabbing in the garbage before let alone, taken the risk of poking around in someone's trash. I couldn't help it, I had to grab the cool carrying case, with all its cowboys and Indians painted on the top. Even if it was empty, I could at least store some of my own toys in it I thought to myself. Then I grabbed the handle, and it was really heavy! I flipped the latch, opened the lid, and low and behold, it was packed to the gills with small cowboys, Indians, horses, wagons, and a ton of other stuff. I couldn't believe it, why would they throw this out?! I grabbed the case and started jogging back home with the biggest smile on my face, spilling my drink all along the way; that moment was unforgettable for me, and after that, I always did a little recon on garbage day and found tons of other great items. That day, I was sold on picking and it changed my life, by setting a whole slew of events in action, which propelled me forward. In these pages, I will share all the secrets that I have learned from that first score at 7 years old, up until this very day. Nothing is promised in this world, including our next breath, but I will give you the tools as I know them, and I hope that this book gives you some inspiration to follow your dreams, find some happiness, and maybe even make a few extra bucks.

Chapter 1

Where to Find the Gold

And the street of the city was pure gold – Revelation 21:21

My grandmother used tell me that, "The streets are paved with gold." What does that mean, you might ask? It means that one man's junk truly is another man's treasure as they say. I'm going to tell you one of the biggest secrets of where all those collectables and resellables come from—the trash! Yes, you heard that right, but there are a multitude of places where all these secondhand items come from. I'm going to include the most commonly profitable areas for prospecting, and it's up to you whether or not each one is your *cup of tea*. This is the down and dirty truth of the industry, so here it goes. There are seven main areas that all items come from, and this will be where you find the gold:

1. The trash

2. Garage sales.

3. Thrift stores.

4. eBay or similar ecommerce Lots

5. Flea Markets

6. Storage units

7. Bulletin Boards

Picking the Garbage

We will start off with the trash, because this actually is where more collectables come from than you would expect. This is by far the most controversial part of this book, and you have to be totally driven and fearless to pick the trash, but the things you will find if you do are unbelievable at times. No matter what anyone tells you, this is actually where the term, "picker" came from. Picking the garbage is really where it all began for a lot of people *in the know*, and eventually picking at a thrift store or flea market caught on as the secondary way of "picking". With all truthfulness, I have picked or have witnessed my picker buddies right next to me literally pull watches worth over a $1000, collectible toys, glassware, coins, and jewelry worth $1000's of dollars right out of a black trash bag or soiled old carboard box in the trash. At first glance, most people would think that these items MUST be stolen, but I have seen it with my own eyes, time and time again, that high value gold, silver, and just about everything else gets tossed in the trash without a second thought by a large amount of the population. Don't believe it? This is the truth, and it is the basis for every single second-hand preowned item on the market. People either know what it's worth and won't part with it, or they just don't care, and would rather donate it to the thrift, toss it, or keep it as an heirloom.

Before the dawn of the internet, garage sales, estate sales, and garbage picking were the main areas from which most items hit the secondary markets like the flea. There needs to be a disclaimer here, garbage picking's legality varies from city to city. There are some places where there are no ordinances, others where you can actually get a license for a small fee from the city to pick the garbage, and yet others where it is illegal, and if caught, you will be ticketed. So, if dumpster diving isn't in your plan, that's ok. You can add this section to your knowledge arsenal, because at some point in the game, you will encounter items from the trash.

You might have seen those guys driving around in rusted out pickup trucks on garbage night, with the back trailer filled to the brim with water heaters, folding chairs, and just about everything but the kitchen sink. Most of those guys are "scrappers", they pick up scrap metal items like refrigerators, cast iron, brass, and just about anything that they can take to the scrap yard to sell off at spot price to make their cash. Some of these scrappers will cross over and grab a piece of antique furniture if they see it, or stumble across a tree lawn where someone is moving or has passed away. If they find a box full of collectables, of course they will grab it. There is a whole science and philosophy to garbage picking that will land you better odds of finding the gold. The first situation is when someone is moving. We have all driven past a front yard that is packed with endless bags, boxes, and furniture out front, and maybe you even had the courage to stop and grab an item or two, throw it in your trunk, and speed away fearfully like a pirate. But the best items in this case are usually bagged up or in those closed boxes. If you are brave enough to start opening some of the boxes or poke a hole in the side of the bags, you can take a quick peek, and see if there are any valuables. In some cases, you will drive past a pile on garbage night, or even better, before dinner time when they first put it out on the tree lawn, and see about 10-20 bags boxes, and furniture. If you don't act right then and there, and I can guarantee you that if you wait till dark, and drive back later, it will be gone. At that point, the pile has usually been ransacked, pillaged, and stripped of anything good. If you find a few good items, poke around and see some old toys, glassware, electronics, or anything of value, you literally have to just start grabbing the other boxes and bags and load them into your vehicle to be sorted out later at home.

Most of the biggest and most profitable piles will be from one of the following situations:

1. Leftovers from a garage or estate sale that didn't sell.
2. The owner of the house has passed away, and their family doesn't want the hassle of reselling the house's contents.
3. The owners are moving.
4. The owners just moved in, and they decided they don't really need all the junk they just brought with them.

Now all these situations apply to any income neighborhood, but let's be honest here...the best piles come from neighborhoods that are mid-high income, especially new builds or rural farm type areas. In the suburbs, you will find some great stuff because, usually there is a greater level of generational wealth there, people have lived there for a few generations, so they have built up quite a bit of junk and inherited items that eventually hit the trash, thrift store, or secondary market. In areas where new houses are built, you will surprisingly see people throw out all kinds of flat screen TV's, blue ray players, video game systems, high-end furniture, musical instruments, sporting equipment, lawnmowers, snowblowers, and just about anything they get tired of looking at. They are financially secure, and they would rather toss things in the garbage than worry about making a few bucks or giving it away. For them it's just a hassle. That's where pickers come in.

In the rural or farm areas, you will find some of the best older type items, like furniture and collectables. Usually, they have lived in those houses for generations, and from time to time, they throw away some very interesting collectables and useful items. A lot of the old timers will talk amongst themselves, and I don't know how many times I have heard the same truthful phrase repeated, "If we didn't save these items from the trash, guess what? They'd be in a landfill for the rest of time". That phrase is so true—do you know how many valuable items are literally sitting under a ton of waste in a city dump never to be found? I could probably write an entire book about garbage picking, but I just have to let you know, that a lot of those people who set up at the flea market or sell on eBay, just found their items in the trash the week before they sold them to you!

Garage Sales

Speaking of front lawns, this is another one that many pickers will swear by. I have bought a 50-piece $2500 antique sterling silver flatware set for $60 at a garage sale. The scrap price alone for the set would be $1400 if you just took it to the local coin shop. I have scored giant Tupperware bins full of vintage toys for $20, that were worth well over $1000. I have found Roseville, Rookwood, and green Vaseline/uranium glass pieces and entire sets for $10 that were worth $100's of dollars, sometimes even for just one piece. You can do just the same! Jewelry, watches, lawncare equipment, the sky is the limit with yard sales, there is just one thing: You have to get there first. Granny used to say, "the early bird gets the worm", and that is true throughout this entire industry. Check the local listings in the paper or social media posts, to find out when the sales are, and plot out your course to be there first thing in the morning.

Sometimes, if I know there is a citywide yard sale, I will map out the streets the night before, that will make it easier on the morning of the sale.

In some cases, there will be a lot of competition, and there will be a line of pros waiting to beat you to it, other times, you will be surprised to find that you are the only one in line at 8am. This will give you first dibs. There are a few important things to know here...if you do find a sale that has some great stuff, and you clean them out, make sure to also ask them if they have anything else that they haven't set out yet, and see if they would be willing to sell it to you. You can give them your phone number or card and follow up later. I have had this payoff bigtime before, and sometimes if they sell a bunch of stuff on the first day, they will also start digging around the house and decide to part with some even better items once they see the money flowing in. Just in case, I sometimes check back the next day at the same house to see if they have any new items on the tables.

I should mention here also that estate sales fall into the garage sale category, the main difference being that estate sales are more regulated. Anyone who has a garage, can have a garage sale, but estate sales usually occur when someone has either died or inherited the property. Usually with estate sales, you will have lawyers involved in this process. There was a time when some friends of mine were involved in the estate business, and we worked with a lawyer who made her main money from clearing estates from start to finish. This is important, because although you may have heard some stories of estate sale gold, the reality is that most of the items are already marked up to a point where the profit margin for you the buyer is not worth it. Now that may not always be the case, you could come across some estate sales that are run by the family, that completely cut out the middleman, in order to avoid all the hassles, and make more profit for themselves. One good thing to know about estate sales is that after they are over, guess where all the unsold items usually go? You guessed it—the tree lawn on garbage day! In those situations, you may find a bunch of decent items that are on the low end, as well as some bigger functional furniture that didn't sell, and yes, it will be free as long as you don't get caught or chased away. In our case, the lawyer would hire us to appraise the entire contents of the house, and then she would facilitate the sale. After the sale was over, she would then hire us to clean out whatever was left. We could take whatever we wanted and toss the rest. If you are so inclined, appraising and liquidating estate sales may also be a means of income for you. There are days when you'll hit the jackpot with garage/estate sales, and other times when you'll come up dry, but that is why you want to diversify the areas that you hunt. That way you'll have multiple streams to fish from.

Thrift Stores

Thrift stores have become a staple in the picker biz, and for good reason, they can definitely pay off big. Before the advent of social media, there was a golden age of picking, and you could find unbelievable valuables being given away for next to nothing, BUT even with all the competition and available technology, you can still find items for resale every week at your local goodwill, Salvation Army, Purple Heart, etc. Now we'll start with some of the main problems, and then we'll talk about the gold. One of the biggest problems is that some store employees/managers think everything is worth a million dollars, so they mark it so high that you can't make any money. These people are ringing you up at the cash register, and then you go ahead and tell them, that the $2 piece of glassware you just purchased is really worth $80. Don't do this—I know it's hard! When you find something awesome, you almost can't help but brag about it. But never, never, ever, tell the cashier, store manager, or the person walking past you your secrets, because guess what, they just might start getting those great items before you do. Now that they know, they might tell everyone else they know in a text message, and then the party's over. I have seen this in action, when there was a "regular" in line, who told the cashier that the painting they just bought for $5 actually was worth $50 for the antique frame alone. And guess what happened the week after? They started marking all the cheap paintings/prints up to $20. Everyone is watching the picker shows, and they think that a $10 watch is worth $50 now, or they think that every junk toy is a collectible, every piece of glassware is Victorian heirloom, and every vase must be from the Ming Dynasty! Just a word of caution here, you may be tempted to still buy those items marked up, thinking that hey, maybe you still make a $20-50 profit. That may be the case, but I would advise you to make a hard pass, and wait for a bigger profit zone. If you can buy 4 items for $1 and turn around and sell them for $5 each, that's not bad, but try and find those items for $1-5 dollars that you can at least make $20 or more from. This keeps your upfront investment low, and if it takes a while to sell, then you aren't out of a lot of cash. If you decide to go big, and pay say $50 for an item, then you definitely:

1.) want to make sure that item is really going to allow you to double your money with a $100 or more profit.

2.) And isn't going to take you forever to sell.

If that's the case, then it becomes part of your collection of junk. It happens to the best of us, but definitely try to spend low, and sell high with everything.

Being the first one at the thrift store doesn't always work out in your favor. Sometimes, you get there right after they open, and an attendant will wheel out a cart of fresh items before they even reach the shelf, while other times they won't put out anything new till after lunch or even dinner time. With the thrift stores, there are certain days that they schedule to restock, and I would casually ask the cashier as you are checking out, which days those are. This will give you a bit of an edge. I have walked in at the most random times of the day to a Goodwill expecting to not find much, only to find a high dollar item on the shelf at an empty store. One time, I walked in and found a green uranium glass decanter with 4 shot glasses, I looked at the tags and saw $3 for the decanter, and $.50 a piece for the glasses. This particular set wound up being a rare Fenton that was worth around $350!

When I enter the thrift, I usually spend about 30-45 minutes in the store, and I hit all the main areas that I know have paid off for me. It's basically a game of finding the items that the store doesn't know are worth anything yet. Sometimes, if the store is understaffed, you will find better items, because lets face it, it's a job, and they just don't care. They are looking at those 20 bins of junk, and they don't have the time to look things up, so they just start marking them at low prices. Those stores are the best, and you will find them by trial and error.

Once everyone hears about that lost copy of the US Constitution that was found in the back of a painting for $3, they think every painting is worth a fortune. So, like all stock markets and financial areas, you want to watch the trends that are selling, and stay ahead of the competition and the store managers. I will personally hit one area of clothing first, and that is to find coats/jackets. This has been an often-overlooked item, that still pays off fairly well at the thrift. You can buy some coats for $5-10 dollars that will easily sell for $80 and up on eBay or other markets. Sports, military, and high-end fashion coats off-season are the best. Check the inner maker tag, and do a quick check on your phone for the value, and grab it if there's a profit to made. I hit glassware, toys, electronics, books, tools, and furniture as well. All those areas can pay off big time.

There is one sad truth that I should mention about thrift stores—some employees and even managers are skimming off top. They will start texting their friends and family who are in the parking lot, just before they put a cart out. In some cases, I have seen that they got fired for stealing from the store itself. But the proof to me that they aren't all on the take, is that I have quite a few stores where I continually, usually weekly, find great items that they missed. So even if they are rigging the system sometimes, you just have to stay one step ahead of them and find those good stores, and niche markets that they haven't figured out yet.

eBay & Ecommerce Sites

You might be thinking that eBay and other similar sites are played out and couldn't possibly be a place to make a profit or find good items to resell, well, I'm here to tell you you'd be wrong, and here's why. Another huge secret to this whole industry is the "Piece it Out Method." In its simplest form, you buy large lots that are higher priced, and then you sell each individual part for more money. There are people who make their entire careers off of this one single method or variations of it. The way this works is this: No matter whether you are bidding on an auction lot consisting of 1000's of sports cards, a 100-piece glassware set, a vintage toy collection with 100's of figures, if you outbid the rest you can then sell each individual item for more. Now this is within reason, and you don't want to spend too much of course, but here's the deal, most people will bid on a large lot just because they want one or two items from the auction, once the price goes too high, they are out. You will see the powerseller eBay dealers doing this. They will buy out a lot for $150 that most people don't have to spend, outbid everyone, and turn around and sell 50 of the items individually for $5 each for a grand total of $250 dollars. Most sellers just want to make the quick buck, and they'd rather just sell the big lot for less and let someone else piece it out. We will revisit these methods in more detail in Chapter 3.

    Drop-shipping is another method that gains small payouts but allows for minimal work. The concept is this: you see a vendor on Amazon or eBay selling

Bluetooth earbuds for $5, you then list those same earbuds on your eBay for $10, once you sell that item, you immediately purchase it from the vendor selling it for $5 and then plug-in the name and address of the customer who just purchased the earbuds from you. You never touch the item, you don't package it up—you never even owned it, but now you get paid. These are just a few ways to find things on eBay and similar sites like Amazon and Temu.

Flea Markets

Even with all the competition, TV shows, and technology, the flea markets are still a gold mine, and yes on a good day with the right tactics you can score big. There are a couple of different types of flea markets: the inner-city junk fest, the suburban arts and crafts, and the rural farm markets. Of the three, the rural farm markets are usually the best, and even though the pros are set up there, you will find what you are looking for whether you are a buyer or a seller. The inner-city junk fests are usually new items or low-end junk with a smaller percentage of possible decent items. The suburban arts and crafts rummage sale type markets that you sometimes see at local churches or community centers can sometimes have an item or two, but if you are looking for the good stuff, I would avoid them in favor of the rural country flea markets 9 times out of 10. Now, don't get me wrong, if you go to the local rummage sale on day one, when they first open before anyone else gets there, you might find a few decent items; but I have found that year after year compared to the flea markets, they are pretty skimpy from my experiences. The arts and crafts shows may have a few antique items for sale, but they will usually be overpriced. This may be, however, a place for you to resell if that is your style. At those types of markets, you will have the advantage as a seller, and you can price high.

Storage units

You've seen the shows, you've seen the characters, and maybe you want to try your luck, well, let me tell you the truth. I have done storage units, and I know people who own their own auction houses, and their main income is from buying storage units, and walk-ins. The storage unit biz is on the decline bigtime. You can still make a profit from time to time, but here is the reality— it's super-competitive, and it's played out. There are a few reasons why there is a huge amount of competition in this arena, and it has drawn quite a few unscrupulous characters. You used to be able to actually bid on, and more times than not, outbid the rest, and get yourself a goldmine or two. Those days are mostly over, and here's why. The first reason is that the market is cornered no matter where you go. There are only so many storage units around, and the big players, auction house owners, and even inside swindlers have the monopoly. It's kinda like the stock market! But seriously, I recently talked with a friend who has been in the business for decades, and his bread and butter came from a certain storage facility that was family owned for over 50 years. They decided to sell it and retire to Florida. Much to my friend's surprise, when he started winning storage unit bids under the new owners, there were some huge changes. He would see the unit, make a cost evaluation, bid, win, and he thought it was all good. Once he was given access to his winning units though, he found that some of the items that he had made note of were missing, and a large number of the boxes that filled the unit were empty. To put it lightly, the units were filled with literal trash. As it turns out, the new sketchy owners were rigging the units and, "cherry picking" the good stuff, and then selling the trash and empty boxes to the highest bidder. Is that illegal? You bet—but when has that ever stopped anyone in the past? Now you will find these types of characters throughout the industry, so be on guard, but we'll talk more about that in Chapter 5. You can try storage units at your own risk, but just watch out for the scammers, and take cell phone pics of everything before you bid.

<u>Bulletin Boards</u>

This has really been a great one for me, and so many other people I know swear by it. In this age of high-tech instant cell phone access, one of the best things you can do is target the people who don't use social media. There are many people who barely use their phones, they are retired, and they still look at those bulletin boards wherever they may be found. Of course, word of mouth in your own social circles is a great way to start. Letting friends and family know that you are looking to buy collectables or items for cash will always start to make some people start digging through their attics. There are a few places where I have consistently placed ads and gotten some great results. You can place ads in your local newspapers, city bulletins, grocery stores, or just about any social clubs for a very small price or free. Always say that you are offering cash for any items from 1 piece to an entire collection, even broken items. A quick sidenote on this, there are some items that are very rare, especially old toys, glassware etc. Even if one piece or a part is broken, you can still use the rest to make a complete collection or repair an item. I have found that this is also in your favor financially because you can offer the seller a lower price if the items are damaged. If something is completely trashed or unsalvageable of course you won't want to buy it, but if there is a $5 Barbie doll with a broken arm, but the outfit she is wearing is worth $100 then by all means make an offer.

Pinning your business cards or flyers with tear-off phone numbers to grocery store, community center, or social bulletin boards can pay big dividends in the end, even if you only get one decent response. Generally, I expect to get a few calls every time, but I have had times where I got five so-so calls, and then there was that one call from a person at an old farmhouse, who says they have some old toys or collectables that they want to get rid of—that's when you hit the jackpot. From there, you can meet/greet, get a little cash flowing, and start asking about all the other items they might be willing to sell. Always ask them if they know anyone else who might want to sell, after your first meeting. This has definitely led me to entire collections for sale in the past. One thing I never do though, is ask if they know anyone else before I have met them in person. This I do from past experiences that didn't go so well. I have driven out to meet people and see their collections, only to find out that after I have arrived, they decided to change their mind, and save the best parts of the collections for themselves. This doesn't always happen, but from time to time, once people start digging through their old stuff, they get sentimental, and only want to part with the lower grade items. When you get that first phone call, I can't stress enough how it is a make-or-break situation. Its your one chance to make a connection with the person, gain their trust, and let them know you aren't a serial killer, before you come to their house or designated location to appraise and buy. I always wait until I find out that they are, "good to go" before I ask them if they know anyone else, because, at that juncture, I have seen them start to call other people, and then they turn around and say that some of those people (their mom, grandma, brother, etc.) said that they shouldn't sell their items because they might be worth more money! So, make the call, set the time to meet asap, appraise on site, and bring cash to buy, before you branch out to their other possible acquaintances.

Now when I first started out doing this, I would drive out alone to remote farmhouses in the middle of nowhere, and meet all kinds of people—some good, some not so much. I know the thought of doing this conjures up images from horror movies for some of you, and that's a good thing. In this day and age, I would recommend that you always bring a buddy with you when you meet someone for a possible transaction. A lot of pickers will meet in the local library parking lot, or even McDonalds to do a trade or sale. Both are perfectly legal and there are usually other people around who can see what's going on. In the case of checking out someone's huge collection, you will most likely have to meet them at their house if they are willing, otherwise, you risk missing out on a lot of the good stuff. If someone tells you they have a huge barn, basement, or attic full of collectables they are willing to sell, you probably don't want to just check out a few items in the Burger King parking lot—you'll miss the best stuff. Time is of the essence between the call and the meeting. To be honest, the longer you wait, the more chances they will have to change their mind about selling some of the items, and I have had some people just back out of the deal entirely. Sometimes you can tell on the phone that it's just a nice old, retired couple, who want to get rid of some junk now that their kids are married and have moved on. Other times though, I have been the one to back out of meeting and appraising at someone's house because, something just didn't seem right. If that's the case, definitely trust your gut instinct—they'll be other times with better items, and in my opinion, you can't be too careful these days.

Antique Shops

The last place I would mention is antique shops. Some antique shops will literally have the best items you will ever find, but, you are going to pay out the wazoo for them. Before the dawn of the internet, a lot of these mom-and-pop shops operated under the tax radar, but now they are quite sophisticated with online auction tie-ins and personal eBay sites. Vendors who rent one of the many stalls at these shops will pay a high premium just to get a small space behind the glass cabinets let alone a booth of their own. You will most likely be required to fill out the tax forms if you decide to rent one of their stalls. Buying at one of these places usually falls into the, "I need this for my personal collection" category rather than, "I can make money off of it." The majority of vendors and owners at antique shops are usually seasoned veterans who know all the tricks, and they are charging a high dollar to prove it. In order to make a profit at an antique shop, you'd better have a lot of stock to sell, and it better be worth a pretty penny. Otherwise, you are just wasting your time. You might have enough stuff to sell for a month or two, but then you'll be cleaned out, and the profit is small. The competition of having 20-50 dealers under one roof means that you most likely aren't going to be finding anything to sell in-house, and any walk-ins are going to go to the owners first. There are some people who thrive in antique shops, but usually they are retired, have saved up their collections for a lifetime, and aren't hard-pressed to sell as much as some people tend to be. If you fall into this category, I salute you for making it this far! If you become the eventual owner of an antique shop or storefront, you'll pretty much hold all the cards, and people will come to you weekly with nice items that they want to sell for cash, just like a pawn shop. Opening a storefront has its pros and cons for sure, but that's a story for another day.

Chapter 2

The Items That Sell

So, you've started to collect or amass a bunch of items to sell, but you aren't sure where to start. In this chapter, we will talk about the main categories that are bankable staples in the picker biz. Whether you sell on eBay, at the flea market, or you open up a store front, the items in this chapter make money. We will start with antiques in general. There are countless price guides available today concerning the antique market, but there are two areas where you will be able to make the most cash: furniture and pottery/glassware. Now, one consideration for both these items is that they are usually fairly heavy in weight. This can be a big mistake that people make when they start out. If you have your own storefront, then this may not matter so much, but if you plan on selling things online or carting them off to the flea market, then size and weight are definitely going to be a big consideration.

I had a friend who found an antique cash register that she wanted to sell—the thing was awesome. It was constructed of solid wood, brass, and metal, and it had all kinds of internal bells and gears. She listed it on eBay, and it sold for over $300, then reality set it...She had to ship it across the country. Even with the economy ground shipping, she ended up paying more than she had into the register and she lost all of her profits entirely. She also had to take a considerable amount of personal time to construct a box made of something more sturdy than moving boxes, and this was also an unexpected expense. The whole transaction should never have happened online. Large furniture like art deco, Victorian, and Civil War era sets can net you big bucks, but you will have to either list them as a "Local Pickup" only or haul them out to the flea market—that is if you have a vehicle big enough. If you have an economy car, a lot of these options just won't fit, and you'll have to pack smaller items.

You'll see the pros at the market bring their larger vehicles just in case they buy a larger item. I have had this happen plenty of times when I first started out in the biz. I would see an old full-sized standup arcade machine for

$75—I knew it was worth $300-$400, but I couldn't fit it in my car! In the time that it took me to think about a million ways to tie it to my car roof, while holding on to the rope and driving at the same time, someone else swooped in, threw it in their truck and drove off. So, an SUV, van, or truck are definitely something to consider if you want to go big and expand your picker horizons. You can still sell a lot of items from an economy car though.

The Depression Era items like glassware, pottery, and medium fixtures such as lamps are all great starting points to enter into the market, but shipping for these items can be a lot more unless you sell them as individual pieces. Pottery items like Rookwood and Roseville are very sought after, and they can easily reach over $100 a piece if they are in nice condition and unrepaired. Ceramic and porcelain figurines like Hummel and Dalton also have their value. The market goes up and down in all these areas, but they consistently maintain a solid value. There are rare pieces in all these pottery figurines that I have seen net in the $1000's of dollars. Search eBay for any item you intend to sell and plug in "Rare" and "Highest Price" to see what they might be worth. I have found Hummel figurines worth several hundred dollars at the Goodwill and Salvation army for $2-5 that were worth anywhere from $25-$225 on occasion.

There are a lot of knock offs for these items as well, so make sure to check the marks on the bottoms to be sure that they are authentic before you buy. There is an endless number of possibilities in the antiques realms, from fountain pens, some of which actually have sterling silver and sold gold tips, to old tin promotion signs like Coca Cola and more. Pick up a few antique guides from your local library, and you will see how far this category can go. Having even a small personal library of price guides is a must for everyone who resells.

Collectible toys are one of the hottest markets at the time of writing this book. This spans the era of pre-WWII tin toys, 1950's cowboys, 1960s -70s Marx, Star Wars, Barbie, and Gi Joe's. There are also a multitude of subcategories that break off from each one of these. In the 1980's Hasbro released a new line of Gi Joe's that were 3 ¾ inch in size to match the other action figures on the previous decades like Star Wars, Battlestar Galactica, Buck Rogers, Clash of the Titans, and many more. Anything from these eras is considered to be one of the golden ages of toy manufacturing.

In recent decades, there have been endless remakes and knockoffs as they are called, and these may look exactly like the originals, so you always have to check the date and manufacturer for these toys when you find them in the wild. Most toys figures from 12-inch Gi Joes and Barbies, to 3 ¾ inch figures usually have a date and manufacturer stamped on their back, legs, or bottom somewhere. Always check for this. Older toys will be stamped: USA, Japan, Taiwan, or the Philippines, while anything made in recent decades will almost always be stamped "Made in China". That's not to say that all toys manufactured in China aren't worth anything, and even many of the 3 ¾ figures from the 1980's and up were made in China, but the older stuff will never be marked "China". There are amazing, licensed reproductions of the original, Star Wars, Marx playsets, Gi Joes, and Barbies, all of which were made in China; They are still collectible and hold some value, but just be on the lookout; what you think might be a $150 figure might actually be a $20 reproduction. At the time of writing this book, Late 1980's - 1990's toys are starting to go through the roof in price and demand. Teenage Mutant Ninja Turtles, Transformers, Ghostbusters, and the final years of the Gi Joe's are all getting top dollar if they are in good shape. Like everything in resale, the better the condition, the higher the price. If you have a vintage item loose and in undamaged condition, then you can get a fair price, but if it is in mint condition with its original packaging, you could easily get much more. We will cover condition and its effects on price in the next chapter, but just so you know how important this difference is, a loose Star Wars figure with its accessories could be worth $8-20, but if it is in the original package unopened, you could possibly be looking at a $500-$2000 value or more...seriously!

Vintage electronics like old tube radios, record players, boomboxes, lamps, and just about anything electrical to make your living space look awesome are all in high demand. Once again, weight can be an issue, but old lamps by Fenton, or ones made out of green uranium glass can fetch upwards of $500 to $1000's of dollars. A lot of the market for these types of items can just be in the selling of replacement parts. Items like rubber belts for turntables and motor driven electronics, tubes and small electrical components, and the glass, brass, or iron parts of the lamps are all in a market of their own. Broken items can usually be fixed or modified into something new with the right pieces. Vintage lamps where the main fixture is a statue are also something to look out for. Art Deco style, or any niche collectible bust like horses, animals, or religious figures are always a good bet. One thing to consider with electronic or battery-operated items is the obvious question...does it work? You might think that this isn't a big deal at first, and many a picker has been tricked into buying a really cool item that they took home, and found it was electrically fried. Always plug the item in to see if it works first.

Watches are a huge seller, whether it is a newer smartwatch or a vintage mechanical automatic, timepieces of all sorts fetch huge amounts of money in the market. Here is a crash course in watches that will keep you from being stuck with junk or buying a fake. There are several types of watches on the market: Automatic, Mechanical, Quartz, and newer rechargeables. Automatic watches will be stamped either on the back or on the face of the watch. These can be, at times, the most valuable of all the watches that you will find. Rolex watches for example are automatic, meaning that they do not need a battery to run. There is a reason why Swiss Rolex automatic watches cost so much, and that is because they are handmade and built to the highest specifications to keep accurate time merely by the motion of a person's wrist while wearing the timepiece. The arm movement of the average person throughout the day, jogs the internal parts of the watch and automatically sets in motion all the gears, springs, and components. Omega brand watches can easily fetch in the $5000-$10000-dollar range, while some Rolex watches can start at about $12000 and up these days. Here's the thing, these watches used to retail at $500-$1000, 20 to 30 years ago, and like many collectible watches, most people got them as a gift or self-reward, and they have no idea of the actual current value.

If you find an automatic watch, and you pick it up, you will usually see the *seconds hand* moving smoothly around the time face. If this is not the case, gently tilting the watch back and forth in a shaking motion 5-10 times should be enough to start the movement and see the *seconds hand* start to turn. If you try this and the *seconds hand is* still froze in place, then it could be broken, or need to be professionally serviced at a watch shop. Now just because an automatic watch is broken or needs to be oiled professionally does not mean it is worthless; A broken Rolex or Omega Moon Watch could still be worth thousands of dollars just for the parts. If you come across one of these in broken condition it may still be worth paying a little more up front if there is money to be made. There are many other automatic watches on today's market that you can buy like Citizen, Seiko, and even Timex, to name a few, and at your local dept store you will pay around $250-500 for these brand-new on the shelf. So, if you find one for $5 at a goodwill or garage sale, grab it, you won't be disappointed.

Mechanical watches are usually wind-up watches that also do not need a battery. A lot of people confuse these with automatics, but they are definitely different internally. These watches need to be wound every day in order to keep time, and they will also be stamped on the face or back of the watch with the "Mechanical" designation. One problem with these watches is that because they need to be wound every day, sometimes the owner overwinds them, and they are stuck. Depending on the make or model, these may or may not be worth fixing. Many of the character watches like Mickey Mouse, Disney, and various cartoon personalities were mass produced in the 1950's-1980's in mechanical versions. A lot of times they will be broken, and there are people who can fix them, but the cost will usually be more than the value of the watch itself. If it's a rare piece, but it is frozen, there may still be some value, but usually it's just a $5-20 range items. Most watches like this will be mass produced but there are still military and WWWII era wind-up watches worth $1000's even in broken condition. Just in case, check before you buy.

Quartz watches are usually your run-of-the-mill cheapo watch that makes up much of the general market. There are however high dollar quartz watches like Citizen, Timex, and many other brands that still retail for over $200 brand new. With quartz watches, always check to see the brand, serial number, and condition before you buy.

Vintage clothes are another incredibly easy market to get into. You may have seen those people at the thrift going through every single shirt, jacket, and pants isle, loading up their carts to the brim. This is a serious market that you can start small and work your way up. Yes, there are Levi's pants worth $100's if not $1000's of dollars that have been found at the local goodwill, and there is a wide variety of styles to choose from. Vintage clothing from the early 1900s to modern sports jackets can be found for under $10 at times and can be resold for $25 and up. Always check the tag and maker for fakes, and make sure there are no holes or stains in the garments. Jackets themselves are a great market to get into, and some stores are starting to catch on to this trend but like all things, they can never catch everything, and they won't sell if they price their coats too high. Vintage wool jackets or cashmere items are good items to look for. Not every wool coat is worth $50, but there are many that are worth much more. In the case of wool, buy brand names that have been around for decades like Woolrich, this will increase the probability of your items selling. You can grab those for $5-$8 at times, and they list in the $50-150 range depending.

Women's vintage clothing is always good. There are many styles and eras that are always marketable, like the 1920's Downtown Abbey, hippy 1970's, 1980's New Wave, and grungy 1990's attire. Official sports team jackets and jerseys, as well as musical tour shirts are all big bucks if they are original and not modern-day reproductions. Military jackets like winter parkas, and some camo can also be bought in the $8 range and resold for $50-$120 at times. There are some dealers that just do shoes, like Air Jordan's, 1980-1990's, and modern fashion like Uggs. Shoes are definitely one of the items that a lot of people avoid just because of the sanitary aspects, but if it's in good clean condition, and you list 3 or 4 pairs that you spent $20 on, you can make $80 or more profit if the market isn't flooded.

Military Items are always hot, but it is not a market that everyone enjoys. From every war that mankind has waged, there are relics, uniforms, and weapons, which tell the tale of the battles fought, won, and lost. Some military enthusiasts just want to collect items like patches and uniforms from their time in the service, while others are historical buffs that chronicle and reenact the battles themselves. Whatever the case, some military items have huge value on the market these days. The items with the most value in recent years are from,

WWI, WWII, Vietnam, and the American Civil War. In all these wars, the uniforms, belt buckles, watches, holsters, and just about any gear that is still surviving is worth money. A lot of the Vietnam era gear can be hard to verify for authenticity because it crosses over into the post-war 1970's issued gear, but there are some items like watches, and even non-government issued items that fetch big bucks. The Seiko "Willard" dive watches from that era can range from $800-$500 because they were worn by some vets during their service. Any official Jackets, uniforms, and gear issued from WWI-WWII are now antique historic items, many of which exist now only because they have been passed down as heirlooms. Leather flight jackets from WWII even in tattered condition still high dollar values if they have been painted with the bomb group on the back or sleeves. Some of these items are purchased and curated by film-prop companies who shell out large amounts of money for set pieces and reproduction guides. There are some items in militaria that are priceless but, but it is a niche market, it's not for everyone.

The last two categories that I would like to mention here are collectible coins and sports memorabilia. The sports industry is multi-billion dollar throughout the world, and there are endless items to sell. There was a time when sports trading card shops existed in nearly every city, and although their numbers have dwindled, the online demand for trading cards is off the charts these days. One thing to know about sports cards and any collectible cards, whether it's Topps baseball, football, or Star Wars, is that there is a grading system, and there is definitely a secret racket in this market. Allow me to introduce to you the PSA trading cards grading system. Let's say you are the owner of a 1969 Topps Reggie Jackson rookie card. You could sell your card in decent condition on eBay for $80, or you could get it graded by a professional and it could be worth $599 or more. There are cards being sold in lots every day for under $100 on eBay that are then sent to be graded, and their value is then authenticated at $1000's of dollars. This goes for every kind of trading card from sports to Star Wars to Pokémon—it makes no difference. This is where collectible coins come in. You may have a coin that you could sell on eBay as a novice that goes for $25, but that same coin could be purchased by someone that authenticates it for a higher value—a MUCH higher value. Trading card and collectible coin grading is a mysterious and at times seemingly sketchy market, much like stocks or any other thing of supposed value, but what it comes down to is, what do you say something is worth? There is no doubt that grading services are legit. All types of collectables can be graded, and you may have seen these types of items on eBay from time to time at ridiculous prices. Allow me to demystify the process for you. It all comes down to this, if you want your $100 carded 1977 Star Wars figure to be worth its actual $2500 value, you have to pay for it. You can join a grading service for a fee, and then, based on the assumed value of the item that you want appraised, graded, and certified, you will pay up front to have your item graded/certified. If your $100 item is really worth $1200, you may pay half that to get its value certified. There will then be a large profit margin for you, but you will pay a bit for it beforehand. Now this, like many things, is where the wealthy get wealthier. This is a HUGE secret in the market. This is what separates the *Big Fish* from the *Small Fish* as they say. Many people don't have $1000's of dollars in the bank to get their carded figures, coins, or trading cards graded. Just like most people aren't Warren Buffet, and don't have millions of dollars to invest that will eventually net them a $100,000 profit quarterly. In the case of grading and certification, yes, it does take money to make money. Here is something to consider though, even if you enter this market at the lowest level at first, say, maybe in the $100-$500 range. I want you to go on eBay, type in "graded trading card" into the search, and then select, "Price + Shipping: Highest First". Yep, you will see single trading cards listed for over $100,000 dollars, with multiple watchers. If you actually follow these markets, you will see that many of these items are not only listed for that amount, but they actually sell! How could an ungraded card sell for $100 but a graded version sells for more than a car or small house? It all comes down to the grading system. So, if that seller makes four transactions per year at $100,000 each, they have made $1,000,000 in transactions. This applies to coins as well. You may have a coin that has a "stamp error" on it, but if you get it graded, you might double or triple its value. The world of coins is much like that of trading cards; There are world coins, and then there are United States minted coins. All can be graded. The value of all coins can be broken down into what they were made of, where and when they were minted, do they have any historical value, and finally their condition.

The precious metals like gold, silver, platinum, and palladium that some coins are minted in are worth more than the face value of the coin, and the world market affects these values on a day-to-day basis. It is deeply tied into the stock market and various other global conditions. US Gold coins minted 30-50 years ago might have been worth a few hundred dollars, but now, their precious metal value could be around the $1700-2000 range. You have the value of the coin based on condition and how many were minted in any given year, and then you have the current spot price for the precious metal itself to factor in. If you have the means to get a 1989 Gold American Eagle graded, it might be worth $6000-$10000 dollars. An ungraded coin might only be worth around $2000.

It would be impossible to cover every item that can be sold on the secondary market in this book, but as you will come to find out, the categories that we have discussed here in this chapter definitely can make you money, and the grading system is something to consider down the road if you get a little extra cash, and want to invest in the long term. Now it's time to sell!

Chapter 3

Strategies For Selling

For the sake of simplicity, we will stick to eBay and the flea market as your main avenues for selling. There are endless other places like Craigslist, Facebook Market, Amazon, Etsy, etc, but whether you decide to sell online, or brave the people face to face at the market, the concept is the same. One thing to think about right from the start with selling online or anywhere for that matter is, where are you going to get all your merchandise?

We have covered in previous chapters where to find cool vintage and collectible items, and even how outbidding others on big eBay lots can pay off, but there is one more thing to consider with the online world: foreign sellers.

The bottom line is this, whether you are Target, Walmart, or any other big-name retailer, you are going to have to buy from China. Now I only mention this because it is another big secret in the eBay game. No matter what you are looking for, whether it is a watch band, camera lens filters, earbuds, or any other emerging technology, you can purchase the exact same thing for around 75% less from China on eBay. I am strictly talking about legal licensed merchandise here—not the illegal knockoffs. There are some online dealers who buy and sell strictly using this method, because, of course, you make more money! There are many reasons why most smaller dealers do not want to buy foreign and sell domestically, and we won't go into that, but it is a huge possibility for profit. You may notice that an exact item that someone is selling for $25 is available from China for $2 with free shipping even. Now it will take some time for your item to arrive on a shipping container, but if you are buying large quantities of say, smart watch bands, earbuds, or cellphone cases for 10 cents on the dollar or cheaper, in the long run it pays off. Once again, this is where the big shots make the bigger bucks. If you buy large quantities for next to nothing and get stuck with a few extra, then you'll still be ahead of the game, with very little loss. One thing to say here is that there are emerging trends in the technology market, and the 500 cell phone cases that you bought 6 months ago might not be marketable next month. So, you have to stay on top of what's selling, what's hot, and how many pieces you should buy upfront. If buying outside of CONUS isn't your thing, just keep it local, and there is nothing wrong with that.

So, you see that others have some items similar to yours online, you've watched them, and can see if they are actually selling, or if they are overpriced and going nowhere. The first thing to do is basically tag off of other sellers recently sold items, or off of ongoing auctions that are actually getting bids. So, if you have a Gi Joe that is worth $200, and you see that there is another one just like yours getting bids and ending in a few days, get yours ready to list. Put the competitor's Gi Joe auction on your watchlist, take pictures of your item, and write up your description. You can save your listing as a "Draft", so that when the time is right, you will make it active to get the most potential buyers. Some people will see an item about to sell, and then a few days before the auction ends, they will start theirs in hopes of snagging some of the bidders that don't want to bid to the top. What I have found is best, is to wait until their auction ends, and then 5 minutes after, I list mine. If I see that their GI Joe sold for $100, had a bunch of bidders, and I want a quick sale, then I will tag off of their auction, at $85-$90 say with a "Buy it Now" option. This technique works 9 times out of 10, because someone that was bidding either just missed the end of the auction, or they just didn't want to bid up $5 to $10 more for the item. In this case, you can make a quick sale, and you don't have to wait through a 7-day auction for your payoff. If you have an item that you aren't sure what it will actually sell for at auction, and you don't want to risk selling it for too little an amount, I would always list it for a starting bid of just a little less than you actually want for it. For example, you have a depression glass vase that you can't find on eBay, but you see other ones just like it selling for $100 consistently, but this one just might be more valuable because there isn't another like it. Then I would start the opening bid around at least $100; That way you get your $100, but maybe, just maybe, it is something more valuable or rare and could command a few hundred dollars more. I have seen this work effectively, and sometimes the reason you don't see your exact item is for the simple fact that it actually is rare and more sought after.

In a previous chapter, I mentioned the "Piece it Out" method. Now we will go a little more in depth about this technique with examples that I know work. The concept is this: I know a guy who sells car parts on eBay, he buys a car for $2000 dollars, and then he sells each piece individually...and I mean every piece until all he is left with is a metal shell which he then sells for scrap. This guy doesn't own a junkyard or a car business, he just buys a few very distinct rundown and sometimes immobile models of cars for a low cost. And after all is said and done, he makes around $20,000 per car. How does he do it, you might ask? He sells everything from the door handles to the hubcaps and speedometer as a separate item online. The car is worthless to most people because it no longer runs, but the individual parts are worth thousands. Now, you may have heard about thieves sawing off catalytic converters so they can sell them for $20 at the scrap yard because they contain palladium, and that's true; but for those who are willing to put in the work, hood ornaments, doors, panels, and everything else are worth a small fortune. This is what junkyards do. They buy broken-down cars and fill their acre lots with junkers to sell for parts. The same is true for everything else that you buy in the collectable realm that has more than one part that might break. I'll give you another example: Vintage Marx playsets are a very hot item. There are some Marx playsets like the Battle of Blue and Grey Civil War set that sells for over $500 complete. But, if you sell every one of the figures, accessories, vehicles, buildings, weapons, horses, and trees as an individual piece for top dollar, you will make closer to $900. Now for some people, they just want to make a quick sale, I'd actually say that the majority of sellers go this route. But for those who don't mind listing more items and shipping them out, the payoff will be nearly double in most cases.

Electric components are the same. A vintage radio is worth $150 let's say, but you decide to open it and sell each tube, knob, and the outer shell as a separate piece, and you've once again doubled your money. There are two views to this method. Some collectors cannot believe that you would take apart a perfectly good playset or item and piece it out. The flipside, which I have found to be true, is that a lot of people are really grateful when they can finally complete their collection or get their item in working order because you decided to take one apart and sell it. It's not like it really matters from a money perspective, but from a collector's perspective, some people are against it. This is where buying things that are broken comes in. Sometimes you can buy a broken item with the intent to piece it out with a lot of success for very little investment. This method is huge in the toy world where every action figure, vehicle, and play set comes with endless weapons, parts, and accessories. There are for instance vintage Star Wars and GI Joe weapons that are so expensive, that there is even an illegal market for 3D printed fake lightsabers and laser blasters on eBay. That just shows the supply and demand for such things.

Barbie clothes and accessories are no exception to this, and every collectible toy market has a huge demand for single parts. In past chapters we talked about broken watches, and the face, dials, band, crown, springs; and every single part of a vintage Rolex or Omega watch can be worth big bucks if they are sold separately to someone who needs to do a costly repair. Vintage clothes need replacement buttons, and a Blu-ray player with remote may sell for $25, but the remote itself could sell for $20 and the player for another $20 if sold separately. Glassware sets may sell for $150, but if you piece out the whole set, you'll double your money on a green uranium glass kitchen set where each plate, cup, and bowl are sold on their own. This concept creates an entire subclass of buying and selling online and at the flea market. There are the flea market sellers who would rather sell a $300 item to you for $100-$125 cash because they want to bother with computers and eBay. You on the other hand are going to pay the eBay and Uncle Sam piper, but you'll still net a higher profit. In some cases, if the price is right, you can walk up and clean a whole flea market table out on a good day and be ready to sell online for a huge profit. You and the dealer have both made your cash, and you both go home happier than when you drove up.

This may be a good time to briefly mention selling fees. Always consider your overhead before you buy. If you pay $50 for a item that you are going to sell for $100, you can pretty much figure that you could be giving eBay or whatever format you sell on these days upwards of 30% of that. So, is it really worth it? If you can grab a $100 item for $10 or $15, then you are in the better profit range. After you've spent your time packing and boxing an item up, and then driving to the post office to ship it, you've spent a considerable amount of time getting from purchase to sale—to the final payoff, so keep those things in mind. If you become a "Power Seller" the people at the post office start knowing you by name, and you can print your postage directly from eBay, and make less trips to the post office by timing out your shipments. Postage can be a great mystery when you first start selling online, but the main thing to know is that international shipping doesn't really pay off unless you are moving big dollar items. Shipping costs are generated automatically through eBay based on package dimensions, weight, and zip code, so definitely measure and weigh your items before you even list them, and factor in your box/envelope costs as well. Online selling is an ever-evolving market, and once you get started, you will begin to see patterns of what is hot and what is not. Some items will fizzle out, only to rise in price the following year. The outdoor flea market is a whole other creature all together, and once you dive in, you'll see what I mean.

Chapter 4

Setting Up And Buying At The Flea Market

The flea markets draw all kinds of folks, from the Amish families selling wonderful food and handmade items, to the diehard business dealers selling knockoff brands of Nike, Calvin Klein, and even Rolex. Like any place that involves money, you will find the best and the worst of humanity. Now, I don't want to scare you, (I'll save that for the buyers beware chapter!), but when you go to the flea market, regardless of whether you are buying or selling, you better get ready to play, and have your poker face on. Some people love the flea markets, some people just go for the exercise they get by walking around, window shopping, and not even buying anything. There is everything under the sun at most markets. Some rural markets even have firearms and ammunition laid right out on the table, as well as various other knives and weapons. The tri-state markets of Ohio, West Virginia, and Pennsylvania sometimes have livestock like cows, goats, sheep, and even horses. These things draw lots of people from far and wide with lots of cash to spend. In the case of the larger markets, some people have driven several hours with the hopes of spending quite a bit of money and making a day of it. In the smaller farm markets, you may see the same faces over and over week after week, with very little money flowing. You'll find the good ones as well as the bad ones once you start visiting them, and there are some that you'll never want to see again.

Setting up at most markets is fairly easy. At some markets you can book your spots online, while others, you just show up and wait for the fee collector to stop by your table and ask for the $10-$20 fee. Some markets are so packed and in demand, that you'll need to call, or fill out their online reservation form a few weeks to a month in advance. You may decide to go all in at some point and rent a permanent booth if you find yourself making money and setting up a few times a month or more. You are definitely going to want to invest in at least one decent folding table. I would suggest two tables. A few rectangular card tables are good, because they can fit in a economy car, whereas longer banquet tables will only fit in larger vehicles. They do make longer rectangular tables that bend in the middle to save space while transporting. Sometimes you can get tables at garage sales, and most of the ones I have ever had, were garbage picked. The older vintage tables are lighter and more compact, if you can find them, and they just look more retro. If the weather is dicey, you don't want to have to lay your items on the grass, or on towels or cardboard, where they will get damaged. There are some mornings where the dew and frost are still on the ground when you start setting up, and this is common, so get a few good tables and save yourself the hassle. Another indispensable but commonly forgotten necessity is plastic shopping bags. I save all my bags from the grocery stores in a bigger trash bag, and then use them at the markets, and for packing items on eBay. You will find that just about nobody seems to bring their own bags to the markets, and when somebody buys a bunch of stuff from you—they either have to learn how to juggle or use a bag.

Whether you are buying or selling at the market, if you expect to find anything good, you are going to have to get there before the competition, at the *crack of dawn.* If you don't follow this rule, you will most likely just be getting the leftovers that the vultures didn't want. If you decide to sleep in and go a few hours late, you might find a thing or two, but the best items will literally be found as the dealers are unloading their cars and setting up their tables. Now here is an important point about this first "morning swoop" as I call it. You will have two types of dealers: the old pros and the new people who have either never set up before or have only done it a few times. You want to find the new dealers as they are setting up their wares. This is where you will hit the jackpot quite frequently. New dealers who are eager to make some money will start selling all their items for low prices because they are getting swarmed by the vultures and think that if they don't accept an offer right then and there, that they might not sell an item at all! This couldn't be farther from the truth. If you have a top dollar item, and the right people are there, it will usually sell. As they are setting up and pulling things out of boxes, dealers and buyers will start haggling over the items, because they know they can make a quick purchase and turn around and sell it at their table for more. This is where you will also find a lot of items that people don't know the actual value of. I have seen huge boxes and lots of old Star Wars toys, glassware, and just about anything you can think of bought for $20 from a dealer before they can even set up; the real value of those items was in the $100's. You would be surprised how many people don't do their research. There are actually still people out there who empty out their attics, go to the market, and sell it all without knowing what it's worth. I am amazed by this fact year after year—and at garage sales as well.

Depending on the size of the market, I will make a quick swoop and scan through a couple of isles or the whole line of tables if I am just buying, then I will go through, and make a more thorough walk-by after I have scored some good items. After you have found some of the good markets out there, you will start to see some of the same dealers and get to know where the good stuff is. Even with some of the pros, who set up week after week, once you start buying from them, they will usually cut you a deal if you are a repeat customer.

If you are setting up, and you get swarmed by buyers as you unload, don't just give your stuff away for cheap to make a quick buck. A lot of people will make a lowball offer, both in the morning, and after a few hours thinking that you might be getting desperate to sell. The thing is, they really want the item if they keep coming back, so stand your ground a little bit, and try to get a higher price. After an hour or two, if you have some items that aren't super-valuable, you can accept lower offers. It'll be less junk that you'll have to take home and unload.

You will encounter some people who aren't so nice. They will try and offer you $10 on an item that you are asking $50 for, and yes that is an insult most of the time. Don't fall for it. Hold the line—don't lose your cool, and just kindly tell them something like, "well, I have $40 in it already so, I'm gonna need to get $50." Some people will actually get a little irate and say that it isn't worth that much or they could get it on eBay cheaper. That may or may not be true, but it's your item; you don't owe them anything, and they can take it or leave. I have actually seen fights start at the market plenty of times over this exact scenario, and it's ridiculous, but some people are just grumpy all the time.

So, let's talk a bit about pricing at the flea market. Now a lot of people will price their items at 50-75% lower than they could be purchased on eBay. The dealers would sell the items themselves that way, but they either aren't tech savvy, or they would rather just make the quick cash. Depending on the market, and items that you have, you should be able to get around 80% for your stuff at the market. Now if you have a rare item, you will have no problem getting top dollar at some markets. I have seen some people walk up to a table, and purchase upwards of $1000 worth of merchandise, load up their truck, and come back for more. Most flea markets though, the buyers are just bringing between $20-$100 or so in personal cash. Some people never bring more than $20, so that's your target range for selling most of the time. The small rural markets usually play out this way. The bigger multi-state markets along the borders will bring people who have driven a considerable distance, and they will usually bring a bigger wad of cash. Make a list of your items throughout the week and write down what range you'd like to sell them for. Take that with you to the market, and you'll be surprised sometimes how close you were to your original estimates.

There is one huge factor with buying and selling at flea markets, and that is the weather. Some markets are seasonal, and they only start setting up in the fields once the winter weather breaks. Others have the best of both worlds, and they have their year-round indoor vendors to fall back on during the rain or snow. Sometimes, you will be watching the weather the night beforehand just to see if it's going to be worth setting up at all. There will always be some vendors and buyers even when the temperatures drop below 50 degrees in some states. That's definitely not for everybody, but you can find some great items during the off seasons, because people are very eager to make a buck, as they are used to making a lot more during the spring and summer. This can also be a good time to sell, because there is less competition. You will have to brave the elements though.

It should be mentioned here also that you want to prepare for your day at the market. You should dress in layers even during a summer day, because in the mornings it will be cold and frosty. It's kinda like a mini camping expedition depending on your vehicle. So, bring snacks, and something to drink to keep your energy up. A side note on camping, it can actually be fun if you buddy-up and bring a friend or two, and camp out the night before. Some places even allow you to have a campfire on the premises. Some vendors will spend the night at a nearby local campground the night before and party it up. If that's what you are looking for, it can be a fun way to make a weekend out of it.

Even if you are setting up for only a few hours, you can get sunburned and really dehydrated. If you don't have an umbrella to set up above you, you can plan on being in the elements from 8am-noon for example. A good sunscreen and sunglasses are a necessity on those days. Some dealers will make their quick cash and leave at 9 or 10, but even after that amount of time, the heat or cold can be a bit exhausting for some. If possible, you should always have a friend to set up with. Let's say you are setting up alone, you've had your coffee, and you've been there for a few hours, you will have to use the restroom. If there is nobody there with you, then you'll either have to walk the distance to restroom in hopes that you don't get ripped off, or you could ask one of the vendors next to you to watch your stuff until you get back. I wouldn't advise doing this, unless you know them really well for obvious reasons. These are the things that you don't think about until you are sitting in the sun on an 80-degree day, people are asking you prices, and all of the sudden you need a restroom brake pronto! Other than that, you can set up how you want, ask what you want pricewise, and you'll probably find that it is kinda fun talking to different people throughout the day about collectables, antiques, and just about anything. If you have business cards made, this will also be a great way to network with other buyers and sellers. There have been plenty of times where a quick conversation at the market or collectable show has led to a bigger opportunity to buy a collection or sell a few items. That is one of the aspects that draws quite a few people to the markets—the common social bond of collecting.

Chapter 5

Buyer (And Picker) Beware

Most people within the United States don't like to sell outside of the country because of customs, forms, and well...getting ripped off. It happens, and I knew a vintage guitar collector/dealer who owned a music store, out of which he would also sell guitars through his eBay account for $1000's of dollars—that was until he started getting ripped off. He would ship off his vintage Gibson Les Paul to Europe, collect his money, and think nothing of it—until he got a message asking for a return and refund from the buyer that is. The lesson here is that there are definitely some scammers in the picker biz, and you want to be on your guard. I have had things stolen from my tables before from flea markets, but I will admit that it is fairly rare. Getting ripped off as a buyer at the market is a whole other story though.

One tactic that some vendors use at the flea market is the, "fill the box scam." This one happens a lot, and it gets even the best of us at times. It goes like this: you see a box full of old collectible toys, and they are asking $100 for this full box, and you see maybe 1 or 2 great items on the top of the pile. You kinda dig around in the box, and it looks like you could make some cash off of this lot. You keep staring at those one or two nice items on the top, and your adrenaline starts pumping, and you just have to buy it. BUT, once you get the box back to your car or house later on and take everything else out and start inspecting your goldmine, you realize that just about every item, including the best one on top, has some major flaw that you didn't see. You just bought "fool's gold." Maybe it was a chipped item, or an electric piece missing a battery cover, or once you turned an item at the bottom of the box over, you could now see that it was broken. In short—you've been had, you just bought a junk box or scrap box of items that you can't sell for what you thought you could. A lot of times with these scams, you will find that all the items in the box have already been stripped of their useful parts, and pieced out before they landed in your hands. What you are left with is worth less than you paid, even if you piece it out.

Since we are talking about subpar junk that you don't want to get stuck with, we should mention here, that there are two things you should always ask yourself before buying something: If broken, would you still be able to display the item you are thinking about buying, and is the item still functional? Some items like glassware or pottery are rare, and even though they are chipped, they can be professionally repaired, or even restored with kits from your local craft store. The problems start to arise though, once you have 3, 4,5—10 of these cracked/chipped items that nobody wants, and you never fix them. One, you should never try to fix an item and sell it as if nothing is wrong with it. This is hopefully obvious to everyone, but I know that I have bought items before only to find out that somebody rigged them with duct tape or super glue just enough for me to miss it until I got home. Don't do this! If there is a chipped item, point that out to the buyer ahead of time, unless it is very minimal.

It is sometimes expected that antique and vintage items may not be fully working because of their age, but with other things it is not. Anything that has a zipper, like coats, pants, shirts etc, you should always check first before you buy. This may seem obvious, but most people get that rush when they find that cool vintage clothing item, only to get it in the car and realize the zipper is ripped, stuck, or nonfunctional—after they paid full price! This happens a lot at the Goodwill and Salvation Army. They probably don't do it intentionally, but I have countless times seen a great jacket worth over $100 in the thrift for $5, then I checked the zipper, and it was ripped. Always plug in electric items to check if possible, and most markets have cheap batteries available to test items. If you overpay for a clothing item with an unfixable zipper, or get a chipped piece of glassware, or broken electronic component, it's pretty much scrapped if you were planning on listing it online. At the flea market you could junk it out and maybe get your money back if you can't sell it for parts, but that's about it. One rule for eBay and online selling that you should go buy, is to only sell items that don't need repair. You just end up practically giving them away if you try. You will see some eBay sellers say, "Untested" in the description, that means— "I tested it, it doesn't work, but hey, give me your money anyway." If somebody is selling an item for $25-50 and they are trying to con you into thinking that they didn't check it with some batteries from the Dollar Store, then I've got some silver-plated flatware that you might want to buy at sterling silver spot price—just let me know.

That brings me to another pothole that many people fall into—sterling silver vs silver plated items. I seriously don't know anyone in the business who hasn't fallen for this at some point early on in their adventures, so I am going to save you some time and money, and let you know, that if that fork, plate, bowl, or whatever it is, isn't marked "sterling silver" or .925—don't buy it unless you check the markings first. Now there are endless websites online that have curated every single type of sterling silver marking in creation, and I even have a printout cheat sheet that I leave in the glove box sometimes, for such occasions. You don't have to be a precious metals expert to keep from getting scammed by the Goodwill or flea marketer. There are a couple of exceptions to this, but they are rare, and that is where doing a little research will pay off. You will see some items, like candle holders that are marked "weighted sterling" and those actually are sterling silver, and they can be sold for scrap, or for a little more as a collectible item. The thing is, weighted silver items are filled with various things like plaster or even hard plastic, leaving only a very thin layer of sterling silver on the outer shell. Unlike plated sterling items, that are basically worth buying for their appearance alone as an actual utensils, weighted silver will be purchased, broken open, and then they will peel the silver layer off to melt down for scrap. Just make sure to realize that a weighted sterling candelabra that is a few pounds, is probably only an ounce or two of actual silver. This varies depending on the object of course, but the main thing is, the actual weight of the item you buy will not even come close to the final spot price of sterling that is stripped from it. A lot of people will see a bag of silver flatware, forks, and spoons in a bag at the thrift or flea market, turn it over, and if they don't see the words, "plated" or silverplate" will still think there is a chance that they just bought a couple hundred dollars' worth of sterling for $20. I'm here to tell you, that probably won't be the case. There are very few markings on silver items other than "sterling silver? that will denote the actual precious metal, so if it isn't marked accordingly, don't even bother, unless you plan on being stuck with a dinner set that you can personally use.

    I have from time to time found a random sterling fork, bowl, or other oddball item at the Goodwill for a few dollars before, but those days are getting fewer and far between as they get wiser to different silver items that might actually be valuable. I have seen an actual sterling silver platters at the thrift in the $5 range before— the marking was on the inner edge, almost unnoticeable unless you carry an eye loupe or magnifying glass. If you flipped it over, it appeared to have no markings at all on the bottom, but on that inner rim, plain as day, it was marked sterling. So, check the edges, inner rims, etc, and you may find a small marking almost hidden. Some antique and vintage dinner knives are marked this way. The blades are stainless steel, and they will be marked accordingly, but the handles, sometimes are sterling, and they will be marked somewhere on the handle. At times, it is so small that you almost need a magnifying glass to see, but it's there. One good thing to have in your pocket at all times, is a small jeweler's eye loupe or magnifying glass. You will see some of the pros at the market and thrift whipping them out and checking the backs of jewelry, watches, and silver items. You'd be surprised how many times sellers miss markings at garage sales, and you can score gold, silver, and even platinum jewelry at junk prices. I have found 14k items in $5 dollar grab bags at Goodwill. You may look at that bag, and see a bunch of costume jewelry, which may be worth something, but sometimes, you can see the markings through the bag, and low and behold, they missed it beforehand. So, the takeaway for all possible precious metal items is this, don't buy if it isn't marked—don't even take the chance on that gold piece of jewelry or silver item, unless you see the mark.

There is some great costume jewelry out there that is worth a pretty penny, and that is a huge market in and of itself, but it's not precious metal. I will let you in on another secret though— there are however some costume jewelry items that are made out of green, clear or uranium glass that will glow under a blacklight. Those items will sell well, and you can purchase a UV flashlight for under $10. Carry one of those around with you, and you'll be able to check depression glass items to see if they glow, and if they do, they are valuable. At the time of writing this, there is a whole TikTok social media trend where people are getting into uranium glass. One aspect of this is that prices are going higher, so there is a new generational market that didn't previously exist. The other side is that there may be more competition to find items for a period of time. Some people think that the cat is out of the bag and the market will crash, but I'm still finding good pieces consistently at the thrift and yard sales.

So now it's time to talk more in depth about the actual physical and legal dangers of the game. We briefly talked about this in previous chapters, but here is the reality: I have had picker friends get tickets for going through the garbage on people's tree lawns, because the owners called the cops. One such incident involved a friend of mine, who found a "moving pile" one Sunday night.

He padded the bags down, opened a few boxes and found a jackpot of collectible items. He valued the score at several thousand dollars once he got it home and sifted through it with his wife. He went back an hour later and literally grabbed every other bag off the tree lawn, and in that round, he found quite a bit more, not thousands of dollars, but at least $300-500 dollars of quality stuff to resell. So, during the whole next week, he'd cruise by the house after dark, to see if there was anything new that they threw out, but he found nothing. Then Sunday rolled around, and lo and behold, the boxes, bags, and old furniture filled the tree lawn again. As he and his wife started tossing everything into the back of their pickup truck, they were interrupted by the local police, who promptly asked them if they had permission to remove those items—which they did not. He gave them tickets without a warning and told them that he never wanted to see them driving around that neighborhood again. Now some of you are reading this and thinking, *yep that's not for me, I would never do that*; but for those people who have been garbage picking for many years, they know that sometimes the risk may pay off, because it's just going to go in a land fill anyway—right? I would recommend that you don't take the risk. As mentioned previously, there are many cities where you can actually get a license to "prospect" garbage from the tree lawn for a small fee, and that is actually an amazing deal. If you do it the legal way, then you are perfectly free to grab whatever you want from any garbage pile in the city.

    Now most people have grabbed an item or two from a tree lawn without much hassle, but the problem comes when the vultures descend on your front lawn, tear the bags to shreds, and leave a huge mess that the owner wakes up to the next morning on their way to work. Nobody wants that, and who wouldn't be angry to have that happen? So, if you do decide to pick the garbage, you definitely want to be respectful of the owner. In many cases, you might even see them in their yard, and just ask them if they mind if you grab an item or two off the top. I have done that for years, and most of the time, they are kind and willing. I've even had them help me to lift heavy furniture into the truck before. But sometimes, you will meet some very angry people. I know pickers who have been yelled at, chased, and even had things thrown at their vehicle, for picking in somebody's yard. One guy was even waiting in the bushes in the dark in full camo one night when me and my friends were picking through his pile for a second week in a row. He yelled at us, but also saw that we were harmless—after that, we never went back to that house! Also, if you pick the garbage enough, you may find things in the bags that you'd wish you'd never seen before! There might be some nice glassware on the surface, and you grabbed the whole bag thinking that was all that was in there, only to get it home, and find out that the bottom was filled with cat litter, dead mice, racoons, or worse! You can use your imagination here to fill in the gaps—I've probably seen it before.

Another big danger is the competition. Like anything that involves money, people will go to great lengths to destroy what they see as a hindrance to their livelihood. On garbage night you will definitely see the same rusted out trucks driving around, making their routes to either get scrap or pick, and I have also seen people get in yelling matches as they drive by telling others that this is their turf. In reality, its nobody's turf. It's all either public or private property, and within the bounds of the law, it's anyone's game. First come first serve really. Now I'll admit, at times, we all get angry when we see somebody find an item before us at the market, thrift, or wherever; but after dark, on the city streets, garbage pickers and scrappers can get a little more hostile from what I've seen. My advice is to just stay clear of those kinds of interactions. If you see somebody picking the road you are on, then skip over them a few streets, and try to hit the ones they haven't hit yet. It's not unusual to see 3 or more people out picking on any given night. When it comes to garbage picking, do a drive-by around dinner time while it's still light out to find the bigger piles, which usually will have started to accumulate earlier, and after dark, you find the smaller piles. Some people are just rough all around, so whether you are in the thrift or on the tree lawn at !2 AM, be kind if you can, and sometimes you'll even make a friend or potential lead to another score in the process!

Chapter 6

What It Takes to Survive

Market trends are always changing no matter what area you might invest in. You should always be looking to expand your horizons to new items that might be of value. Some people just like to stick to one or two types of collectables, because that is where their knowledge or expertise is at, but there are so many other avenues to resell, and why limit yourself. Another thing to consider is that every market eventually has its downturn. I've seen some toys or antiques go sky high, then 6 months later, they go cold. During that downturn, they usually maintain some solid value—it's not like the floor totally bottoms out, but things that were selling for $300 can drop down to $50 sometimes if the market gets flooded—and eventually it does. You can do one of two things at that point—sell out what stock you have for a lower price or wait until it hopefully gains value again. Comic books went through a long period where some of the major issues were red-hot; then they dropped down bigtime, but now, about 10 years later, comic books are fetching huge prices again. There will always be the staples in any collectible market that are ridiculously priced no matter what, like $100,000 comic books, $5000 Pokémon cards, but the in-between items might not hold a steady value once the majority of collectors start filling out their collections to the point where they aren't missing too many items. I have seen some collectables go out of style, because the people who collected them are no longer alive. Entire generations of people may pass away, but then there starts to be a new excitement for retro items collected by younger generations. There was a time when you couldn't give away a lot of the toys made from the 90's, but now—lookout, they are worth top dollar for some carded and boxed items. Everything seems to come back around again eventually, like the clothes from the show *Downtown Abbey*. A whole new generation of interest in the antique styles of the past has emerged.

To make it in the picker biz, you definitely want to have multiple types of things to sell.

When you think about the profit margins that you can make as you begin, try and keep a realistic expectation. It is true that the sky is the limit, and if you have more money to invest, then you most definitely have the possibility of a bigger payoff, but if you buy too much junk that doesn't sell, then you are stuck with it, and have to wholesale it out. I have seen people buy everything from concert t-shirts to mood rings to sell on eBay and the market. Many of those people invested a substantial amount of money to get going, but once they realized that when you buy 100 concert shirts or 50 mood rings in bulk, you get stuck with odd sizes that nobody wants to buy. The long story short is that the standard sizes sold out quickly, and they made back most of their money, but once they got stuck with the less common sized stock, they sat on it for months, and eventually liquidated the rest. If you decide to buy any item in bulk, keep that in mind. Make sure that you have a choice as to which sizes you can purchase, and if you can't buy 50 items without there being too much variation, don't do it. Just buy smaller sets of 5-10 at the sizes you know will sell. This is what you see even in major retailers around the world. At the end of the season, the markdowns aren't usually in standard sizes that sell as well, and then they start selling things for 75% less than they started with. I would say in the beginner's stage, in order to survive, you definitely want to start with more sure bets. Now if you find that hot item, and it's good to go and it's available, then by all means, make the purchase and flip the stock for a higher rate.

Vintage or antique items on the other hand are a totally different market. Take for example the prices for some carded figures or trading cards that we mentioned in a previous chapter. I'm not even talking about graded figures or items now, just good to mint condition collectables like action figures, playsets, and boxed vehicles for example. At the time of writing this, there are carded Star Wars, Gi Joe, Teenage Mutant Ninja Turtles, and Pokémon figures cards and accessories that are worth $1000's in their original packages, and they are selling. If you look at these trends, you will see that these items are actually worth more than a lot of the precious metal markets like gold, silver, and platinum. How so you ask? Gold and platinum have been bouncing around at anywhere in between $1200 to $2000 per ounce in recent years, and their value is going up, but it isn't going up $1000's of dollars per year, or even per decade in most cases. Some people think of precious metals as a hedge against inflation, and I agree, it is a good idea if you can afford it, but there are some carded/boxed collectables that were worth $500, 5 years ago, that are now going for $1000's of dollars. Now here is the thing, it is a market, and at any time, it could crash, get flooded, or just become something that loses interest. But if you look at investing in vintage higher range collectables like carded Star Wars or GI Joe figures from the 1970s-1980s, you will see that yes, you will pay anywhere from $50 to well over a $1000, but they keep going up in price because of their rarity, or they at least level off and maintain their value. Like everything, it usually takes money to make money, and if you have $10,000 to invest in gold, and if it goes up just 5% then yes you make $500, but if you have to sit on $500 worth of gold for 5 years, you aren't going to make much of a profit. The collectible market though offers quicker returns on a smaller level. This is how pawn shops clean house when they buy. They have a store front, and people are unfortunately usually in a bad situation, where they are offered 10-20% of the value on items that the shop will quickly flip for more money. The collectible market I think can be a bit more ethical of an avenue. What you decide to buy items for is up to you. Just make sure you are looking at the long-term goal.

There is one thing that I have noticed about people who both sell and collect. They will always start to build a collection of high value items for themselves, and then sell off the lower grade items though the secondhand market. Whether it is antiques, jewelry, toys, or old radios—put some items aside that keep the collector-fire going on inside you. This is one good way to stay motivated when the chips are down. If you have to, you can always sell once items reach top dollar in value, but always keep a few of the nicest items for your own personal collection. This can be a modest beginning; I'm not talking about a $5000 vase. It could just be a quality collection that starts off small, that you can build like a nest egg for the future.

To make it in this biz, you have to expect that, like any endeavor, there will be great days, but also days when you might feel like quitting. One thing you should take into consideration, is what is your endgame or ultimate goal. Are you doing this for fun, to socialize, and make a few extra bucks on the side, or are you seriously looking to build up slowly and open a store front of your own? Look at those goals and expectations and make a short-term plan and an extended 1-year plan, if you are serious about the outcome. With those goals laid out on paper, even if you don't meet the expectations that you had, or decide to take another approach, at least you'll have a guideline to follow along the way to check your progress. Once you have that in place, and you start to see that success is happening, your items are making decent profits, and you are actually enjoying the process, then you can celebrate. Make sure to reward yourself along the way, especially once you make that first big flip on an item. Whether you make $50 or $500, you'll be moving closer and closer to the goals that you have set along the way. To thrive rather than just survive, should always be your main focus, and even when the going gets tough, there's a plan in place to lead the way.

Epilogue

The Treasure Hunt Continues

The search for hidden treasure is deeply ingrained in our psyches. Searching for and finding collectables can become an obsession for some. It can be the driving force that starts a new way of life for you. I have known many people who started off as collectors, who then became traders of collectables, and then eventually decided that they had way too many things, and it was time to sell off a thing or two. There are some who can get into this market and just sell without any emotional attachment to the items, but there are others who truly enjoy selling a quality piece to a person who will finally be able to finish their collection, or maybe even start their collecting journey. I have always thought of it as prospecting like the early pioneers did. There is no greater rush than putting in the work, going out to the market, thrift, or checking out a collection, and finding the big score—you'll know it when it happens, and if you follow some of the strategies in this book, and be proactive—it will happen for you. I can still remember driving home in 1992 from a friend's house at around 3am in the morning and seeing a huge tree lawn filled with old toy boxes from the 1960s mixed in with black garbage bags and boxes. I pulled over with my flashlight, started peering in the boxes, and that's when I saw old 1960's Gi Joes, some Marx tin toys, and vintage Barbies with bags of clothes and accessories. I found the goldmine that night. My car was filled to the brim. What did I pay for all those toys that wound up being valued at over $2000? Nothing—they were free! I saved what I wanted, gave the Barbies to my girlfriend, and the rest is history. Little did I know that it would be a catalyst in my journey that would open up even more doors to picking. The chase really is better than the catch at times, and once you finally find that missing piece, or experience that synchronistic moment that you have been searching for, guess what? It's not time to quit—it's time to find something else to collect or pursue. Whatever you choose to do with this book, I hope that it enhances your joy of collecting, and helps you to avoid so many of the pitfalls and losses that myself and others have experienced along the way. Life is better with purpose, and whether or not you find your true calling in these pages, or just enjoy the read…never stop searching, collecting, and hoping for a better day—it might just be right around the corner.